THE AWESOME BOOK OF CAT HUMOR

BOB PHILLIPS

CARTOONS BY JONNY HAWKINS

HARVEST HOUSE PUBLISHERS

EUGENE, OREGON

Cover by Dugan Design Group, Bloomington, Minnesota

THE AWESOME BOOK OF CAT HUMOR

Copyright © 2009 Text by Bob Phillips
Illustrations by Jonny Hawkins
Published by Harvest House Publishers
Eugene, Oregon 97402
www.harvesthousepublishers.com

ISBN 978-0-7369-2516-7

Printed in the United States of America

09 10 11 12 13 14 15 16 17 / BP-SK / 10 9 8 7 6 5 4 3 2 1

CRAZY CAT RIDDLES

Q: If a cat won an Oscar, what would he get?
A: *An A-cat-emy Award.*

Q: What was the first cat to fly?
A: *Kitty-hawk.*

Q: What do baby cats wear?
A: *Diapurrrrrs.*

Q: What do you call a cat with a pager?
A: *A beeping tom.*

Q: What do cats drink on a hot day?
A: *Mice tea.*

Q: What did the cat say when all the dogs left town?
A: *"Good mews!"*

Q: What do you give a cat that has everything?
A: *A wide berth.*

Q: Why do cats sing in back alleys?
A: *That's shoo business.*

Q: What is a cat's second favorite song?
A: *"What's New, Pussycat?"*

Q: What is a cat's favorite song?
A: *"Three Blind Mice."*

Q: Why do most people like cats?
A: *Cats have pleasing purr-sonalities.*

Q: What do you get when you cross a cat with a hyena?
A: *A gigglepuss.*

Q: What do you call a cat that doesn't get its feet wet?
A: *Puss in boots.*

Q: Who is the heavyweight boxing champ of cats?
A: *Muhammad Ali-cat.*

"I'm not going up there—it's a dogwood."

Q: How do you stop a ten-pound parrot from talking too much?

A: *Buy a twenty-pound pussycat.*

Q: What did the cat say when it upset the milk dish?

A: *Nobody's purr-fect.*

Q: What did the cat say when someone called it a name?

A: *"That was a catty remark."*

Q: What's the difference between Coca-Cola and a cat washing itself?

A: *One is the pause that refreshes; the other refreshes its paws.*

Q: What animal has the head of a cat, the tail of a cat, and the ways of a cat, but isn't a cat?

A: *A kitten.*

Q: What kind of car do cats like to ride in?

A: *Cat-illacs.*

Q: What is the highest award a cat can earn?

A: *The Purr-litzer Prize.*

Q: How do you spell cat backward?
A: *C-a-t b-a-c-k-w-a-r-d.*

Q: What do cats put in soft drinks?
A: *Mice cubes.*

Q: What do you call a cat in the middle of a desert?
A: *Lost.*

Q: What do you call a cat inside of a thimble?
A: *Stuck.*

Q: When is seeing a cat bad luck?
A: *When you're a mouse.*

Q: What do you do if a cat catches on fire?
A: *Put it out.*

Q: What type of cat should you avoid playing with?
A: *A cheat-ah.*

Q: What do you do with a blue cat?
A: *Try to cheer him up.*

Q: How many cat litter boxes does it take to stink up a room?

A: *A phew.*

Q: What do cats like to have for breakfast?

A: *Mice Krispies.*

Q: How is cat food sold?

A: *So much purr can.*

Q: What do you get if you cross a hungry cat and a canary?

A: *A cat that isn't hungry anymore.*

Q: What do you call someone who steals cats?

A: *A purr-snatcher.*

Q: What big cat lives in the backyard?

A: *A clothes-lion.*

Q: What do they call a person who delivers mail for kittens?

A: *A litter carrier.*

Q: What happened when the cat swallowed a ball of yarn?

A: *She had mittens.*

Q: What do you call a tiny kitten that writes songs?
A: *An itty bitty ditty kitty.*

Q: Why do cats chase birds?
A: *For a lark.*

Q: What TV program do cats watch to keep up on current events?
A: The Evening Mews.

Q: What do you get when you cross a cat with a stove?
A: *A self-cleaning oven.*

Q: What's a cat's favorite side dish at lunch?
A: *Mice-a-Roni.*

Q: What's a cat's favorite dish at dinner?
A: *Mice pilaf.*

Q: What's a cat's favorite dessert?
A: *Mice cream.*

Q: What's a cat's other favorite dessert?
A: *Chocolate mouse.*

"It's the only way I can eat them."

Q: What do cats call mice on rollerskates?
A: *Meals on wheels.*

Q: What magazine do cats like to read?
A: Good Mousekeeping.

Q: What do you call a cat that likes to go bowling?
A: *An alley cat.*

Q: What do cats like on a hot day?
A: *Mice-cream cones.*

Q: What do you get if you cross a cat with a canary?
A: *A peeping tom.*

Q: What did the cat say to the fish?
A: *"I've got a bone to pick with you."*

Q: What do you call a cat that never comes when it's called?
A: *Im-puss-ible.*

Q: Now you see it…now you don't. What are you looking at?
A: *A black cat walking over a zebra crossing.*

Q: What has four legs, a tail, whiskers and goes round and round for hours?

A: *A cat in a clothes dryer.*

Q: What is a cat's favorite television rerun?

A: Miami Mice.

Q: What's furry, has whiskers, and chases outlaws?

A: *A posse-cat.*

Q: What do cats strive for?

A: *Purr-fection.*

Q: What do you call a cat that has been thrown into the dryer?

A: *Fluffy.*

Q: What do you call a cat that gets thrown in the dryer and is never found again?

A: *Socks.*

Q: What do cats call mice?

A: *Delicious.*

Q: Where do cats go for school excursions?

A: *To the mew-seum.*

Q: What has four legs and flies?
A: *A dead cat.*

Q: What do you call a cat who loses a fight?
A: *Claude.*

Q: What you call a Chinese cat that spies through windows?
A: *A Peking tom.*

Q: What do you call a cat's garbage?
A: *Kitty litter.*

Q: Why did the cat put its kittens into a drawer?
A: *It didn't want to leave its litter lying around.*

Q: What do cats say when you step on them?
A: *"Me-OWWWW!"*

Q: How do you call a cat with three heads?
A: *Here kitty, kitty, kitty.*

Q: How do you get if you cross a cat with a gorilla?
A: *An animal that puts you out at night.*

Q: What did the freshman computer science major say when he was told that the work stations had mice?

A: *Don't you have a cat?*

Q: What is a cat's way of keeping law and order?

A: *Claw enforcement.*

Q: How did a cat take first prize at the bird show?

A: *He just jumped up to the cage, reached in, and took it.*

Q: Why did a person with an unspayed female cat have to go to court?

A: *For kitty littering.*

Q: Why did the litter of communist kittens become capitalists?

A: *They finally opened their eyes.*

Q: Why are cats better than babies?

A: *You only have to change a litter box once a day.*

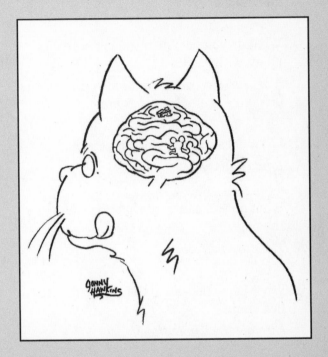

Q: What is the name of a cat's unauthorized autobiography?

A: Hiss and Tell.

Q: What do you get when you cross an elephant with a cat?

A: *A big furry creature that purrs while it sits on your lap and squashes you.*

Q: What does a cat do when it gets mad?

A: *It has a hissy fit.*

Q: What do you call a cat that was caught by the police?

A: *The purr-petrator.*

Q: What happened when the cat went to the flea circus?

A: *He stole the whole show!*

Q: What is a cat's favorite color?

A: *Purrrrrrrple!*

Q: Where does a cat go when it loses its tail?

A: *The re-tail store.*

Q: What do cats use to make coffee?

A: *A purr-colator.*

Q: What do you call a cat that has swallowed a duck?

A: *A duck-filled fatty puss.*

Q: If lights run on electricity and cars run on gas, what do cats run on?

A: *Their paws.*

Q: When is a cat grouchy?

A: *When it's in a bad mewd.*

Q: If ten cats are on a boat and one jumps off, how many cats are left on the boat?

A: *None! They were copycats.*

Q: Is it bad luck if a black cat follows you?

A: *That depends on whether you're a man or a mouse.*

Q: How does a cat get its own way?

A: *With friendly purr-suasion.*

Q: What do you call a cat that lives in an igloo?
A: *An eski-mew.*

Q: What has more lives than a cat?
A: *A frog. It croaks every night.*

Q: What is a cat's favorite subject in school?
A: *Hiss-tory.*

Q: How do cats end a fight?
A: *They hiss and make up.*

Q: What's happening when you hear, "woof... splat...meow...splat"?
A: *It's raining cats and dogs.*

Q: Why are cats such good singers?
A: *They're very mew-sical.*

Q: What do you call newborn kittens who get passed from owner to owner?
A: *Chain litter.*

Q: How many cats can you put into an empty box?
A: *Only one. After that, the box isn't empty.*

"Gesundheit."

Q: Why do you always find the cat in the last place you look?

A: *You stop looking after you find it.*

Q: If a cat can jump five feet high, why can't it jump through a three-foot-high window?

A: *The window is closed.*

Q: What is a cat's favorite movie?

A: The Sound of Mew-sic.

Q: What does a cat that lives near the beach have in common with Christmas?

A: *Sandy Claws.*

Q: Where is one place that your cat can sit but you can't?

A: *Your lap.*

Q: Why did the cat put oil on the mouse?

A: *It squeaked.*

Q: What side of the cat has the most fur?

A: *The outside.*

Q: What kind of cat will keep your grass short?

A: *A lawn meow-er.*

Q: Why did the judge dismiss the entire jury of cats?

A: *Each of them was guilty of purr-jury.*

Q: What do you use to comb a cat?

A: *A cat-a-comb.*

Q: Why did the cat run from the tree?

A: *It was afraid of the bark.*

Q: What looks like half a cat?

A: *The other half.*

Q: What do you get if you cross a cat with a parrot?

A: *A carrot.*

Q: How do cats eat spaghetti?

A: *The same way everyone else does—they put it in their mouths!*

Q: What did the Shakespearean cat say?
A: *Tabby or not tabby!*

Q: What did the cat say when he lost all his money?
A: *I'm paw!*

Q: How do you know if your cat has eaten a duckling?
A: *It's got that down-in-the-mouth look!*

Q: What's worse than raining cats and dogs?
A: *Hailing taxicabs.*

Q: What noise does a cat make going down the highway?
A: *Meoooooooooooooooooooooooooooooooow!*

Q: What do you get if you cross a cat with a canary?
A: *Shredded tweet.*

Q: What does an unlucky cat have?
A: *A cat-astrophe.*

Q: What do you get if you cross a cat with a tree?

A: *A cat-a-log.*

Q: What do you call a cat with eight legs that likes to swim?

A: *An octo-puss.*

Q: Why did the cat join the Red Cross?

A: *It wanted to be a first-aid kit.*

Q: What do cats drink from when they're in space?

A: *Flying saucers.*

Q: Why do cats lick milk out of bowls?

A: *They don't know how to use straws.*

Q: Why did Mr. and Mrs. Cat get married?

A: *They were a purr-fect match.*

Q: What is the difference between a dog and a cat?

A: *A dog will drop everything and come when you call. A cat will check its schedule and try to fit you in.*

Q: What is the feline's favorite baseball position?
A: *Cat-cher.*

Q: What does a cat say when someone pulls its tail?
A: *"Me-ow!"*

Q: What did the angry cat say?
A: *"I'm fur-ious!"*

Q: What do you call a feline's bite?
A: *Cat-nip.*

Q: How did a cat put the iceman out of business?
A: *The cat got his tongs.*

Q: What is another name for a cat's home?
A: *A scratch pad!*

Q: What do you call a cat's table manners?
A: *Eti-cat.*

Q: Where do cats write down notes?
A: *Scratch paper.*

"I used to be Claude—now I'm de-Claude!"

Q: What do you call a cat who eats lemons?
A: *A sour-puss!*

Q: What's a cat's favorite food?
A: *Pet-atoes.*

Q: What's a cat's second favorite food?
A: *Spa-catti.*

Q: What kind of cats lay around the house?
A: *Car-pets.*

Q: What do you call it when a cat stops?
A: *A paws.*

Q: Why do cats get hair balls?
A: *They love a good gag.*

Q: What do you say when a cat finishes sleeping?
A: *Cats-up.*

Q: What do you call a cat who does tricks?
A: *A magic kit.*

Q: Why did the silly kid try to feed pennies to the cat?

A: *His mother told him to put money in the kitty.*

Q: What kind of work does a weak cat do?

A: *Light mouse work.*

Q: Why did the mama cat put stamps on her kittens?

A: *She wanted to mail a litter.*

Q: Which state has a lot of dogs and cats?

A: *Pet-sylvania.*

Q: What kind of baths do cats like best?

A: *Milk baths.*

Q: What do you call a cat penny?

A: *A purr-cent.*

Q: What game did the cat want to play with the mouse?

A: *Catch.*

Q: How do you mail a cat?
A: *Use furs-class mail.*

Q: How do you make a cat dizzy?
A: *Give it a tailspin.*

Q: What do you get if you cross a fence post with a kitty?
A: *A polecat.*

Q: Why couldn't the cat go to the fancy party?
A: *Her fur coat was at the cleaners.*

Q: Why did the cats sell their homes?
A: *The neighborhood had gone to the dogs.*

Q: Where does a cat hang its wash?
A: *On a fe-line.*

Q: Why did the dog and cat go "toot, toot"?
A: *They were trum-pets.*

Q: What do alien cats like to have for breakfast?
A: *A flying saucer of milk.*

Q: What do submarine cats use to see when they're underwater?
A: *A purr-iscope.*

Q: What do English cats drink in the afternoon?
A: *Kit-tea.*

Q: Why did Mrs. Cat go to the beauty parlor?
A: *She wanted to get a purr-manent.*

Q: What do you use to spell "cat"?
A: *Kitty letters.*

Q: Why did everyone like Tom Cat?
A: *He was very purr-sonable.*

Q: How do you call a barber cat?
A: *"Hair, kitty."*

Q: Why was the baby kitten so irritable?
A: *It needed a cat nap.*

Q: What kind of cat goes boom, boom?
A: *A tom tom cat.*

Q: Where did the lonely cat run an ad?

A: *In the purr-sonal column of the newspaper.*

Q: What grows in a marsh and meows?

A: *Cat-tails.*

Q: Where did the kittens go on their class trip?

A: *To a mew-seum.*

Q: Have you heard the joke about the cat on the roof?

A: *Never mind. It's over your head.*

Q: What do people in England call little black cats?

A: *Kittens.*

Q: What would you get if you crossed a cat and a donkey?

A: *A mewl.*

Q: What would you get if you crossed a cat and a pair of galoshes?

A: *Puss 'n boots.*

"That's my flea bag."

Q: What would you get if you crossed a dog and a cat?

A: *An animal that chases itself.*

Q: What do kittens like to put on their burgers?

A: *Cat-sup!*

Q: What song do cats adore?

A: *"Felines, nothing more than felines…"*

Q: How do you spell mousetrap in three letters?

A: *C-a-t.*

Q: What did the dog do on Halloween?

A: *Scare-de-cat.*

Q: Where do cats look up library books?

A: *The card cat-alog.*

Q: What do you call a cat surrounded by a hundred mice?

A: *Purr-fectly happy!*

Q: When is a cat most likely to run out of the house?

A: *When the door is open.*

Q: Did you ever see a catfish?
A: *No! How did it hold the rod and reel?*

Q: What do you call a chubby kitty?
A: *A fat cat.*

Q: What do you call a cat who works out?
A: *A fit kit.*

Q: What do you call a threadbare cat?
A: *A shabby tabby.*

Q: What do you call an urban feline?
A: *A city kitty.*

Q: What do you call a cross between a cat and a skunk?
A: *A mew phew.*

Q: What are the last two hairs on a cat's tail called?
A: *Cat hairs.*

Q: What do you get if you cross a kitten and a little girl's hairdo?
A: *A braidy cat.*

"I catnapped on and off all
day...boy, am I tired!"

Q: What would you get if you crossed a kitten with a melon?

A: *A cat-aloupe.*

Q: What would you get if you crossed a kitten and a mackerel?

A: *A catfish.*

Q: What would you get if you crossed a cat and an octagon?

A: *An octa-puss.*

Q: What do you get when you cross a chick with an alley cat?

A: *A peeping tom.*

Q: What do you call four Spanish cats in quicksand?

A: *Quatro sinko.*

Q: Why did the cat cross the road?

A: *To prove he wasn't chicken.*

Q: How did the cat feel after the dog chased it through a screen door?

A: *Strained.*

Q: What did the hundred-pound mouse say when it walked down the alley?

A: *"Here, kitty, kitty."*

Q: What time is it when seven cats are chasing a mouse?

A: *Seven after one.*

Q: What did the witch's angry cat do?

A: *It flew off the handle.*

Q: Can a cat play patty-cake?

A: *Paw-sibly.*

Q: Did you hear about the cat who drank five bowls of water?

A: *He set a new lap record.*

Q: How do you know when your cat has been using your computer?

A: *When your mouse has teeth marks on it.*

Q: How does a cat count?

A: *One, mew, three...*

Q: How does a cat sing scales?
A: *Do, re, me-ow...*

Q: How is a cat laying down like a coin?
A: *His head is on one side, and his tail is on the other.*

Q: In which month do cats meow the least?
A: *February—it's the shortest month.*

Q: On what should you mount a statue of your cat?
A: *A cat-erpillar.*

Q: What cat purrs more than any other?
A: *Purr-sians.*

Q: What did one gossipy cat say to the other?
A: *Have you heard the mews today?*

Q: What did the cat do after he swallowed some cheese?
A: *He waited by the mouse hole with baited breath.*

Q: What did the mouse say when the cat bit his tail?

A: *That's the end of me!*

Q: What does a sour puss eat?

A: *Crab meat.*

Q: What is a cat's favorite party game?

A: *Mews-ical chairs.*

Q: What is white, sugary, has whiskers, and floats on the sea?

A: *A cat-a-meringue!*

Q: What sport do cats play?

A: *Hair ball.*

Q: What works in a circus, walks a tightrope, and has claws?

A: *An acro-cat!*

Q: When the cat's away...

A: *...the house smells better.*

"I didn't realize *how* curious."

"Did you wipe your hands
on the cat again?"

Q: Who helped Cinderella's cat go to the ball?
A: *Her furry godmother.*

Q: Who was the most powerful cat in China?
A: *Chairman Meow.*

Q: Why are cats longer in the evening than they are in the morning?
A: *They're let out in the evening and taken in the morning.*

Q: Why did the cat frown when she passed the henhouse?
A: *She heard fowl language.*

Q: Why did the cat put the letter *m* in the freezer?
A: *It turns ice into mice.*

Q: Why did the cat sleep under the car?
A: *It wanted to wake up oily.*

Q: Why was the cat so small?
A: *It drank condensed milk.*

Q: Why is a thirsty cat like a runner on a track?

A: *It keeps going back for one more lap.*

Q: Why do cats make terrible storytellers?

A: *They only have one tail.*

Q: How do you know that cats aren't over-sensitive?

A: *They never cry over spilled milk.*

"Careful—this is a
high-risk neighborhood."

CLASSIC CAT QUOTES

There is no snooze button on a
cat who wants breakfast.

Thousands of years ago, Egyptians worshipped
cats as gods. Cats have never forgotten this.

Cats are smarter than dogs. You can't get
eight cats to pull a sled through snow.

JEFF VALDEZ

In a cat's eye, all things belong to cats.

As every cat owner knows, nobody owns a cat.

ELLEN PERRY BERKELEY

Dogs believe they are human.
Cats believe they are God.

One cat just leads to another.

ERNEST HEMINGWAY

Dogs come when they're called; cats take
a message and get back to you later.

MARY BLY

Cats are rather delicate creatures, and they are
subject to a good many ailments, but I never
heard of one who suffered from insomnia.

JOSEPH WOOD KRUTCH

People who hate cats will come
back as mice in their next life.

FAITH RESNICK

There are many intelligent species in the
universe. They are all owned by cats.

I have studied many philosophers and many cats. The wisdom of cats is infinitely superior.

HIPPOLYTE TAINE

❀ ❀ ❀

There are two means of refuge from the miseries of life: music and cats.

ALBERT SCHWEITZER

❀ ❀ ❀

Cat names are more for human benefit. They give one a certain degree more confidence that the animal belongs to you.

ALAN AYCKBOURN

❀ ❀ ❀

To bathe a cat takes brute force, perseverance, courage of conviction, and a cat. The last ingredient is usually hardest to come by.

STEPHEN BAKER

❀ ❀ ❀

Cats' hearing apparatus is built to allow the human voice to go easily in one ear and out the other.

STEPHEN BAKER

A dog will sit beside you while you work.
A cat will sit on the work.

PAM BROWN

🐾 🐾 🐾

Guys are like dogs. They keep coming
back. Ladies are like cats. Yell at a
cat one time, and they're gone.

LENNY BRUCE

🐾 🐾 🐾

I had been told that the training
procedure with cats was difficult.
It's not. Mine had me trained in two days.

BILL DANA

🐾 🐾 🐾

Some people say that cats are
sneaky, evil, and cruel.
True, and they have many other
fine qualities as well.

MISSY DIZICK

🐾 🐾 🐾

Women and cats will do as they
please, and men and dogs should
relax and get used to the idea.

ROBERT A. HEINLEIN

I have noticed that what cats most appreciate in a human being is not the ability to produce food, which they take for granted, but his or her entertainment.

GEOFFREY HOUSEHOLD

❖ ❖ ❖

Some people say man is the most dangerous animal on the planet. Obviously those people have never met an angry cat.

LILLIAN JOHNSON

❖ ❖ ❖

Cats are intended to teach us that not everything in nature has a function.

GARRISON KEILLOR

❖ ❖ ❖

I found out why cats drink out of the toilet. My mother told me it's because the water is cold in there. How did my mother know that?

WENDY LIEBMAN

❖ ❖ ❖

Cats are mean for the fun of it.

P.J. O'ROURKE

I gave my cat a bath the other day. He loved it. He just sat there and enjoyed it. It was fun for me. The fur kept sticking to my tongue, but other than that…

STEVE MARTIN

❖ ❖ ❖

A cat pours his body on the floor like water.

WILLIAM LYON PHELPS

❖ ❖ ❖

The problem with cats is that they get the exact same look on their face whether they see a moth or an ax murderer.

PAULA POUNDSTONE

❖ ❖ ❖

You can tell a dog to do something. You can put to a cat a reasonable proposition.

MICHAEL STEVENS

❖ ❖ ❖

One is never sure, watching two cats washing each other, whether it's affection, the taste, or a trial run for the jugular.

HELEN THOMSON

❖ ❖ ❖

If it's raining at the back door, every cat
is convinced there's a good chance that
it won't be raining at the front door.

WILLIAM TOMS

🐾 🐾 🐾

A man who carries a cat by the tail learns
something he can learn in no other way.

MARK TWAIN

🐾 🐾 🐾

A dog is a man's best friend. A
cat is a cat's best friend.

ROBERT J. VOGEL

🐾 🐾 🐾

If a dog jumps into your lap, it is because
he is fond of you; but if a cat does the same
thing, it is because your lap is warmer.

A.N. WHITEHEAD

🐾 🐾 🐾

The cat has too much spirit to have no heart.

ERNEST MENAUL

🐾 🐾 🐾

Time spent with cats is never wasted.

🐾 🐾 🐾

Heaven will not ever Heaven be
Unless my cats are there to welcome me.

🐾 🐾 🐾

You will always be lucky if you know how
to make friends with strange cats.

🐾 🐾 🐾

Cats seem to go on the principle that it never
does any harm to ask for what you want.

JOSEPH WOOD KRUTCH

🐾 🐾 🐾

Cats aren't clean, they're just
covered with cat spit.

JOHN S. NICHOLS

🐾 🐾 🐾

The cat who doesn't act finicky soon
loses control of his owner.

MORRIS THE CAT

🐾 🐾 🐾

In a cat's eye, all things belong to cats.

🐾 🐾 🐾

No matter how much cats fight, there always seem to be plenty of kittens.

ABRAHAM LINCOLN

🐾 🐾 🐾

With the qualities of cleanliness, affection, patience, dignity, and courage that cats have, how many of us, I ask you, would be capable of becoming cats?

FERNAND MERY

🐾 🐾 🐾

How we behave toward cats here below determines our status in heaven.

ROBERT A. HEINLEIN

🐾 🐾 🐾

If animals could speak, the dog would be a blundering outspoken fellow, but the cat would have the rare grace of never saying a word too much.

MARK TWAIN

🐾 🐾 🐾

The purity of people's hearts can be quickly measured by how they regard animals.

✿ ✿ ✿

Of all God's creatures, there is only one that cannot be made slave of the lash. That one is the cat. If man could be crossed with the cat it would improve the man, but it would deteriorate the cat.

MARK TWAIN

✿ ✿ ✿

I like pigs. Dogs look up to us. Cats look down on us. Pigs treat us as equals.

WINSTON CHURCHILL

✿ ✿ ✿

Woman, poets, and especially artists like cats; delicate natures only can realize their sensitive nervous systems.

HELEN M. WINSLOW

✿ ✿ ✿

Managing senior programmers is like herding cats.

DAVE PLATT

✿ ✿ ✿

"I'm serving their eviction notice.
They keep stealing my saucer of milk
and churning it into cheese."

Beware of people who dislike cats.

🐾 🐾 🐾

I love my cats because I love my home, and little by little they become its visible soul.

JEAN COUTEAU

🐾 🐾 🐾

My husband said it was him or the cat...I miss him sometimes.

🐾 🐾 🐾

Garfield's law: Cats instinctively know the precise moment their owners will awaken... then they awaken them ten minutes sooner.

JIM DAVIS

🐾 🐾 🐾

We have two cats. They're my wife's cats, Mischa and Alex. You can tell a woman names a cat like this. Women always have sensitive names: Muffy, Fluffy, Buffy. Guys name cats things like Tuna Breath, Fur Face, Meow Head. They're nice cats. They've been neutered and they've been declawed. So they're like pillows that eat.

LARRY REEB

🐾 🐾 🐾

I got rid of my husband. The cat was allergic.

🐾 🐾 🐾

Cat: A pygmy lion who loves mice, hates
dogs, and patronizes human beings.

OLIVER HERFORD

🐾 🐾 🐾

"Daddy, Daddy—Fluffy is dead!"
"That's okay, dear. Fluffy has gone
to heaven to be with God."
"What would God want with a dead cat?"

🐾 🐾 🐾

I'm not one of those who can see the cat in
the dairy and wonder what she's there for.

GEORGE ELIOT

🐾 🐾 🐾

Ignorant people think it's the noise which
fighting cats make that is so aggravting, but it
ain't so; it's the sickening grammar they use.

MARK TWAIN

🐾 🐾 🐾

One of the striking differences between a cat
and a lie is that a cat has only nine lives.

MARK TWAIN

🐾 🐾 🐾

If a cat spoke, it would say things like
"Hey, I don't see the problem here."

ROY BLOUNT JR.

🐾 🐾 🐾

To err is human, to purr, feline.

ROBERT BYRNE

🐾 🐾 🐾

Two cats can live as cheaply as one, and
their owner has twice as much fun.

LLOYD ALEXANDER

🐾 🐾 🐾

There are people who reshape the world
by force or argument, but the cat just lies
there, dozing; and the world quietly reshapes
itself to suit his comfort and convenience.

ALLEN AND IVY DODD

🐾 🐾 🐾

No one can have experienced to the
fullest the true sense of achievement
and satisfaction who has never pursued
and successfully caught his tail.

ROSALIND WELCHER

🐾 🐾 🐾

I think it would be great to be a cat!
You come and go as you please.
People always feed and pet you.
They don't expect much of you.
You can play with them, and when
you've had enough, you go away.
You can pick and choose who
you want to be around.
You can't ask for more than that.

PATRICIA MCPHERSON

🐾 🐾 🐾

Work—other people's work—is
an intolerable idea to a cat.
Can you picture cats herding sheep or agreeing
to pull a cart? They will not inconvenience
themselves to the slightest degree.

LOUIS J. CAMUTI

🐾 🐾 🐾

A cat sleeps fat, yet walks thin.

FRED SCHWAB

❧ ❧ ❧

In my experience, cats and beds seem
to be a natural combination.

LOUIS J. CAMUTI

❧ ❧ ❧

Never hold a DustBuster and
a cat at the same time.

❧ ❧ ❧

I put down my book, *The Meaning of Zen,*
and see the cat smiling into her fur as she
delicately combs it with her rough pink
tongue. "Cat, I would lend you this book to
study, but it appears you have already read
it." She looks up and gives me her full gaze.
"Don't be ridiculous," she purrs, "I wrote it."

DILYS LAING

❧ ❧ ❧

In order to keep a true perspective of
one's importance, everyone should
have a dog that will worship him
and a cat that will ignore him.

DEREKE BRUCE

❧ ❧ ❧

What is the appeal about cats?…I've always wanted to know. They don't care if you like them. They haven't the slightest notion of gratitude, and they never pretend. They take what you have to offer, and away they go.

MAVIS GALLANT

❖ ❖ ❖

A kitten is chiefly remarkable for rushing about like mad at nothing whatsoever, and generally stopping before it gets there.

AGNES REPPLIER

❖ ❖ ❖

Our words should be purrs instead of hisses.

KATHERINE PALMER PETERSON

❖ ❖ ❖

I always find it curious as to why I take such great pains to keep my cat's dishes clean when I know I'll look out the window and see her happily carrying a dead mouse in her mouth.

FANNIE ROACH PALMER

❖ ❖ ❖

Until one has loved an animal, a part of one's soul remains unawakened.

ANATOLE FRANCE

❖ ❖ ❖

I care not for a man's religion whose
dog or cat is not the better for it.

ABRAHAM LINCOLN

🐾 🐾 🐾

The cat lives alone, has no need of
society, obeys only when she pleases,
pretends to sleep that she may see the
more clearly, and scratches everything
on which she can lay her paw.

FRANCOIS RENÉ CHATEAUBRIAND

🐾 🐾 🐾

There once were two cats at Kilkenny,
Each thought there was one cat too many,
So they quarrell'd and fit,
They scratch'd and they bit,
Till, excepting their nails
And the tips of their tails,
Instead of two cats, there weren't any.

🐾 🐾 🐾

Cats know not how to pardon.

JEAN DE LA FONTAINE

🐾 🐾 🐾

It's better to feed one cat than many mice.

🐾 🐾 🐾

"No, not my dog. I do my homework on my computer…and the cat ate the mouse."

Is it yet another survival of jungle instinct,
this hiding away from prying eyes at important
times? Or merely a gesture of independence,
a challenge to man and his stupid ways?

MICHAEL JOSEPH

If a cat does something, we call it
instinct; if we do the same thing, for the
same reason, we call it intelligence.

WILL CUPPY

Watch a cat when it enters a room for
the first time. It searches and smells
about, it is not quiet for a moment, it
trusts nothing until it has examined and
made acquaintance with everything.

JEAN-JACQUES ROUSSEAU

The fog comes on little cat feet. It sits
looking over harbor and city on silent
haunches and then, moves on.

CARL SANDBURG

I believe cats to be spirits come to earth.
A cat, I am sure, could walk on a
cloud without coming through.

JULES VERNE

🐾 🐾 🐾

I have cats because they have no artificially
imposed, culturally prescribed sense
of decorum. They live in the moment.
If I had an aneurysm in the brain and
dropped dead, I love knowing that, as the
paramedics carry me out my cats are going
to be swatting at that little toe tag.

PAUL PROVENZA

🐾 🐾 🐾

"We delegate all that fetching stuff
for dogs to do."

"It must be my crow's feet."

A lady went into an antique shop, looking for a good deal. While strolling around the shop, she happened to notice a black cat lapping milk from an old saucer that was a very valuable antique.

"I don't see anything today that I particularly want," she told the owner. "But that's a pretty cat. Would you sell him to me?"

"That is a nice cat," said the owner. "But my little boy is very fond of the cat. I wouldn't want to sell it."

"What about twenty-five dollars?" said the lady. "You could buy your boy several cats for that."

"Well, I'm not sure."

The woman responded, "Then how about thirty-five?"

"Oh, well, if you insist. I'll let you have it for that," the antique dealer said with a sigh.

"I might as well take the saucer, too," said the woman as she picked up the cat.

"I'm sorry," said the dealer. "That saucer is

worth a lot of money as an antique. Besides, because of that saucer, I sell an awful lot of cats to people who know antiques as well as you do."

🐾 🐾 🐾

President Coolidge had guests for dinner at the White House, friends from Vermont. They were worried about their table manners, so they decided to watch the president and do whatever he did.

When President Coolidge poured his coffee into his saucer they did the same. When he added cream and sugar they followed what he did. Then the president placed the saucer of coffee and cream on the floor for the cat.

🐾 🐾 🐾

Ding dong bell,
Pussy's down the well,
But we've used some disinfectant
And don't mind about the smell.

🐾 🐾 🐾

They say that curiosity killed the cat.
What in the world does a cat want to know?

🐾 🐾 🐾

Two cats were watching a tennis game.
One said, "My dad's in that racket."

🐾 🐾 🐾

My cat's name is Ben Hur. We called it Ben till it had kittens.

🐾 🐾 🐾

"Did you know there's a black cat in the dining room?"

"Don't worry, they're supposed to be lucky."

"Well, this one certainly is. He's eating your dinner."

🐾 🐾 🐾

Mother: Junior, don't pull the cat's tail.
Junior: I'm only holding. The cat is pulling it.

🐾 🐾 🐾

A cat's motto: No matter what you've done wrong, always try to make it look like the dog did it.

🐾 🐾 🐾

You can tell your cat is overweight when it's run over by a car and the car comes off worse.

🐾 🐾 🐾

"I'm not worried—even if it doesn't open,
I'm confident I'll land on all fours."

A man decided to get rid of his wife's cat, which he really hated. He put it into the car and drove 20 blocks from home and let it out. When he got back home he was shocked to find the cat sitting in the driveway.

The next night he did the same thing, but this time he drove 20 miles from home. When he returned, he was hungry and went to get something to eat in the kitchen. While he was fixing a sandwich, he heard a scratch at the door. When he opened the door, he almost fell to the ground. The cat was sitting there looking at him.

The third night he drove 60 miles from home down back roads in a deserted farm area. He let the cat out and started back home. About four in the morning, his wife received a phone call. It was her husband.

"I know it's late, but could you tell me if the cat is there?"

"Why, yes. I let the cat in a couple of hours ago."

"Would you please put the cat on the line?"

"Why?" asked the wife.

"I'm lost, and I need some directions home."

🐾 🐾 🐾

How to Give a Pill to a Cat

Step 1. Pick up the cat and cradle it in the crook of your left arm as if holding a baby. Position right forefinger and thumb on either side of the cat's mouth and gently apply pressure to cheeks while holding pill in right hand. As cat opens mouth, pop pill into mouth. Allow cat to close mouth and swallow.

Step 2. Retrieve pill from floor and cat from behind sofa. Cradle cat in left arm and repeat process.

Step 3. Retrieve cat from bedroom and throw away soggy pill.

Step 4. Take new pill from foil wrap. Cradle cat in left arm, holding paws tightly with left hand. Force jaws open and push pill to back of mouth with right forefinger. Hold mouth shut for ten seconds.

Step 5. Retrieve pill from goldfish bowl and cat from top of wardrobe. Call spouse from garden.

Step 6. Kneel on floor with cat wedged firmly between knees, hold front and rear paws. Ignore low growls emitted by cat. Get spouse to hold head firmly with one hand while forcing wooden ruler into mouth. Drop pill down ruler and rub cat's throat vigorously.

Step 7. Retrieve cat from curtain rail; get another pill from foil wrap. Make note to buy new ruler and repair curtains. Carefully sweep shattered figurines from hearth and set to one side for gluing later.

Step 8. Wrap cat in large towel and get spouse to lie on cat with head just visible from below armpit. Put pill in end of drinking straw, force mouth open with pencil and blow down drinking straw.

Step 9. Check label to make sure pill is not harmful to humans, drink glass of water to take taste away. Apply Band-Aid to spouse's forearm and remove blood from carpet with cold water and soap.

Step 10. Retrieve cat from neighbor's shed. Get another pill. Place cat in cupboard and close door onto neck to leave head showing. Force mouth open with dessert spoon. Flick pill down throat with elastic band.

Step 11. Fetch screwdriver from garage and put door back on hinges. Apply cold compress to cheek and check records for date of last tetanus shot. Throw ripped T-shirt away and fetch new one from bedroom.

Step 12. Call fire department to retrieve cat from tree across the road. Apologize to neighbor who crashed into fence while swerving to avoid cat. Take last pill from foil wrapper.

Step 13. Tie cat's front paws to rear paws with garden twine and bind tightly to leg of dining table. Find heavy duty pruning gloves from shed. Force cat's mouth open with small wrench. Push pill into mouth followed by large piece of fillet steak. Hold head vertically and pour half a pint of water down throat to wash pill down.

Step 14. Get spouse to drive you to walk-in clinic. Sit quietly while doctor stitches fingers and forearm and removes pill remnants from right eye. Stop at furniture shop on the way home to order new table.

Step 15. Arrange for your nearest animal shelter to collect cat, and call local pet shop to see if they have any turtles.

🐾 🐾 🐾

A tomcat and a female tabby were courting on the back fence one night. He leaned over to her and purred seductively, "I'd die for you."

She looked up coyly and replied, "How many times?"

🐾 🐾 🐾

"I want a cat, but Mom says I have to start with a caterpillar."

10 Reasons Why Cats and Teenagers Are Alike

1. Neither teenagers nor cats turn their heads when you call their name.

2. Cats and teenagers can lie on the sofa for hours on end without moving.

3. Just as you rarely see a cat out walking with a human being, no teenager ever wants to be seen in public with his or her parents.

4. Cats and teenagers yawn in exactly the same manner, communicating a sense of complete and utter boredom.

5. No cat or teenager shares your taste in music.

6. Regardless of what you do for a cat or a teenager, it is never enough. You are there just to feed them.

7. No matter how well you tell a joke, no cat or teenager will ever crack a smile.

8. Cats and teenagers wreck furniture.

9. Given the chance, cats and teenagers like to wander off at night in search of action.

10. Cats have nine lives; teenagers carry on as if they did.

🐾 🐾 🐾

Signs Your Cat Has a Personality Disorder

- He couldn't muster sufficient disdain if all nine lives depended on it!

- You've repeatedly found him in the closed garage, hunched over the wheel of your car with the engine running.

- You find teeth and claw marks all over your now-empty bottles of Prozac.

- He no longer licks his paws clean, but washes them at the sink again and again and again…

- He continually scratches on the door to get in—the *oven* door.

- He doesn't get Garfield but laughs at Marmaduke.

- He rides in your car with his head out the window.

- You realize one day that the urine stains on the carpet actually form the letters N-E-E-D T-H-E-R-A-P-Y.

- He has built a shrine to Andrew Lloyd Webber entirely out of empty 9 Lives cans.

- He spends all day in the litter box, separating the green chlorophyll granules from the plain white ones.

- Sullen and overweight, your sunglass-wearing cat shoots the TV with a .45 Magnum when he sees cartoon depictions of stupid or lazy felines.

- Your stereo is missing, and in the corner you find a pawn ticket and two kilos of catnip.

How to Clean a Cat

1. Thoroughly clean the toilet.

2. Add the required amount of shampoo to the toilet water and leave the lid up.

3. Soothe the cat while you carry him toward the bathroom.

4. In one smooth movement, put the cat in the toilet and close the lid.

    Note: You may need to stand on the lid so that he cannot escape.

    Caution: Do not get any part of your body too close to the edge, as his paws will be reaching out for any surface they can find.

5. Flush the toilet three or four times. This provides a power wash and rinse, which I have found to be quite effective.

6. Have someone ready to open the door to the outside, and ensure that no one is standing between the toilet and the outside door.

7. Stand behind the toilet as far as you can and quickly lift the lid.

8. The now-clean cat will rocket out of the toilet and run outside, where he will dry himself.

Sincerely,
the Dog

Children as Pets

Have you ever realized that children are like dogs, but teenagers are like cats?

It's so easy to be a dog owner. You feed it, train it, and boss it around, and yet it still puts its head on your knee and gazes at you as if you were a Rembrandt painting, and it bounds indoors with enthusiasm when you call it.

Then around age 13, your adoring little puppy turns into a cat. When you tell it to come inside, it looks amazed, as if wondering who died and made you emperor. Instead of dogging your door-steps, it disappears, and you won't see it again until it gets hungry. Then it pauses on its sprint through the kitchen long enough to turn its nose up at whatever you're serving. When you reach out to ruffle its head in that old affectionate gesture, it twists away from you and gives you a blank stare, as if trying to remember where it has seen you before.

You, not realizing that the dog is now a cat, think something must be desperately wrong. It seems so antisocial, so distant. It won't go on family outings.

You're the one who raised it and taught it to fetch and stay and sit on command, so you assume that you did something wrong. Flooded with guilt and fear, you redouble your efforts to make your pet behave.

But now you're dealing with a cat, so everything that worked before now produces the opposite of the desired result. Call it, and it runs away. Tell it to sit, and it jumps on the counter. The more you go toward it, with open arms, the more it moves away.

Instead of continuing to act like a dog owner, you should learn to behave like a cat owner. Put a dish of food near the door, and let it come to you. Sit still, and it will come, seeking that warm, comforting lap it has not entirely forgotten. Be there to open the door for it. And just remember…one day your grown-up child will walk into the kitchen, give you a big kiss and say, "You've been on your feet all day. Let me get those dishes for you."

Then you'll realize your cat is now a dog again!

🐾 🐾 🐾

What a Cat Wants You to Believe
Versus What It Truly Thinks

I am too proud to beg and may appear to be a very independent creature, but I ask for your loving care and attention.

Translation: I'm the boss, serve me.

I rely on you for my well-being much more than you may realize.

Translation: Go out and earn money so I can enjoy a comfortable lifestyle.

I promise I will not be a burden on you, nor will I demand more of you than you care to give.

Translation: The more attention I get, the more I want. (And by the way, I lie!)

I will be a quiet and peaceful island of serenity to gaze on, a soft and soothing body to caress. I will purr with pleasure to rest your weary ears.

Translation: I will tear round the house smashing decorations at three a.m., infect the house with fleas, and bite your mother when she comes to visit. (Did I mention that I lie?)

I am a gourmet who appreciates different taste sensations, so I hope you will give me a variety of nutritious foods and fresh water daily.

Translation: I need Evian water, changed at least six times a day, chilled but not too cold. Any food you buy me, no matter how expensive, will be turned down if I think I can scrounge the three-day-old bread the neighbors put out for the birds.

You know how I love to sleep. Allow me a warm sheltered place where I can rest peacefully and feel secure.

Translation: Don't you dare wake me. I know where you sleep, and I will get revenge.

If I am wounded in battle or suffering from disease, please tend me gently and see that I am treated by loving and competent hands.

Translation: I reserve the right to mangle the most expensive hands you hire to treat me.

Please protect me from the inhumane people who would hurt and torture me for their own amusement. I am accustomed to your gentle touch and am not always suspicious or swift enough to avoid such malicious acts.

Translation: If you accuse me of biting your mother's thumb and giving her tetanus, I'll claim that she woke me up when I was having a bad dream.

In my later years, when my senses fail me and my infirmities become too great to bear, allow me the comfort and dignity that I desire for my closing days and help me gently in my pain or passing.

Translation: When I've had enough of being pampered, please send me to my next life, where I look forward to being satisfactorily served once more.

My dear friend, my fate depends on you.

Translation: I might just accept you as slave if you behave yourself.

🐾 🐾 🐾

24 Cat No-No's

1. I will not flush the toilet while my human is in the shower.

2. I will not puff my entire body to twice its size for no reason after my humans watch a horror movie.

3. I will not slurp fish food from the surface of the aquarium.

4. I will not lean over to drink out of the tub, fall in, and then run screaming into the box of clumping cat litter.

5. I will not use the humans' bathtub to store live mice for late-night snacks.

6. I will not eat large numbers of assorted bugs and then come home and barf them up so the humans can see that I'm getting plenty of roughage.

7. I will not eat my human's pet rat.

8. I will not help myself to Q-tips, and I will not attempt to stuff them down the drain to dispose of them.

9. I will not perch on my human's chest in the middle of the night and stare into her eyes until she wakes up.

10. As fast as I am, I must remember that I cannot run through closed doors.

11. I will not back up off the front porch and fall into the bushes just as my human is explaining to his girlfriend how graceful I am.

12. I will remember that I am a walking static generator. My human does not need my help installing a new board in her computer.

13. Birds do not come from the bird feeder. I will not repeatedly knock it down and try to open it up to get the birds out.

14. I will remember that my human really will wake up and feed me. I do not have to pry his eyelids open with my claws.

15. I will remember that a warm pepperoni pizza is not a good place for a nap!

16. I will not hide behind the toilet so I can pat the human on the backside when he sits down just to make him levitate.

17. I will not drag dirty socks up from the basement in the middle of the night, deposit them on the bed, and yell at the top of my lungs so my human can admire my "kill."

18. If I sit in the sink while my human is brushing his teeth, I will not get angry when he spits toothpaste on me.

19. I will not knead my human at three a.m. with claws extended. It seems to cause him some discomfort, and he wakes up all grumpy.

20. I will not attempt to stop my human's snoring by sticking my paws into his mouth.

21. I will not use my psychic powers to project myself into my human's dreams when I am hungry, causing her to dream that I am a talking cat and that I can say, "Where's my supper!"

22. I will not teach the parrot to meow in a loud and raucous manner.

23. When my humans play darts, I will not leap into the air and attempt to catch them.

24. I will not display my worm collection on the kitchen floor on a rainy night. My human does not like finding it with her bare feet.

🐾 🐾 🐾

TIME MANAGEMENT FOR CATS

What a Mother Cat Teaches Her Kittens

- All rules can be broken when you feel like it.
- Don't worry about vet bills. Someone else will pay.
- Know where the sock drawer is for those cat-naps.
- Help with jigsaw puzzles.
- Sniff every stranger.
- Be astonishingly mysterious.
- When in doubt, chase something.
- Don't play in plastic bags.
- Ignore your mistakes.
- When in doubt, let your tail do the talking.
- Never sleep alone.
- Curtains are for climbing only.
- All chairs belong to the cat of the house.
- Baths are for dogs!
- Feeding time is whenever *you* want to be fed.
- Go absolutely berserk for no apparent reason.
- Scratching humans and furniture is a no-no.
- Try to keep a mouse alive for your human.
- Make the world your playground.

- Whenever you miss the sandbox, cover it up. Dragging a sock over it helps.

- If you can't get your way, lay across the keyboard till you do.

- When you are hungry, meow loudly so someone feeds you just to shut you up.

- Always find a good patch of sun to nap in.

- Nap often.

- When in trouble, just purr and look cute.

- Life is hard, and then you nap.

- Curiosity never killed anything except maybe a few hours.

- When in doubt, cop an attitude.

- Variety is the spice of life. One day, ignore people; the next day, annoy them.

- Climb your way to the top; that's why the curtains are there.

- Make your mark in the world, or at least spray in each corner.

- Always give generously; a bird or rodent left on the bed tells them, "I care."

🐾 🐾 🐾

Simon gave up the leg brush and went to
the more macho greeting—the head butt.

Cat Survival Guide

1. Doors. Do not allow closed doors in any room. To get a door opened, stand on your hind legs and hammer with your forepaws. Once a door is opened, it is not necessary to use it. After you have ordered an outside door opened, stand halfway in and out and think about several things. This is particularly important during very cold weather, rain, snow, or mosquito season. Avoid swinging doors at all costs.

2. Chairs and rugs. If you have to throw up, get to a chair quickly. If you cannot manage in time, get to an Oriental rug. If there is no Oriental rug, shag is good. When throwing up on the carpet, make sure you back up so that it is as long as a human's bare foot.

3. Bathrooms. Always accompany guests to the bathroom. It is not necessary to do anything—just sit and stare.

4. Hampering. If one of your humans is engaged in some close activity and the other is idle, stay with the busy one. This is called "helping," otherwise known as "hampering." Here are some of the many rules for hampering:

- When supervising cooking, sit just behind the left heel of the cook. You cannot be seen and thereby stand a better chance of being tripped over and then picked up and comforted.

- For book readers, get in close under the chin, between eyes and book, unless you can lie across the book itself.

- For knitting projects or paperwork, lie on the work in the most appropriate manner so as to obscure as much of the work as possible (or at least the most important part). Pretend to doze, but every so often reach out and slap the pencil or knitting needles. The worker may try to distract you. Ignore it. Remember, the aim is to hamper work. Embroidery and needle-point projects make great hammocks in spite of what the humans may tell you.

- For people paying bills (monthly activity) or working on income taxes or Christmas cards (annual activity), sit on the paper being worked on. When dislodged, watch sadly from the side of the table. When activity proceeds nicely, roll around on the papers, scattering them to the best of your ability. After being removed for the second time, push pens, pencils, and erasers off the table, one at a time.

- When a human is holding up the newspaper to read, jump on the back of the paper. Humans love surprises!

5. *Walking.* As often as possible, dart as quickly and closely as possible in front of the human, especially on stairs, when they have

something in their arms, in the dark, and when they first get up in the morning. This will help their coordination skills.

6. Bedtime. Always sleep on the human at night so he or she cannot move around.

🐾 🐾 🐾

How Many Cats Does It Take to Screw In a Lightbulb?

Persian: "Lightbulb? What lightbulb?"

Somali: "The sun is shining, the day is young, we've got our whole lives ahead of us, and you're worrying about a burned-out lightbulb?"

Norwegian forest cat: "Just one. And I'll replace any wiring that's not up to date too."

Cornish rex: "Hey, guys, I've found the switch."

Sphynx : "Turn it back on. I'm cold."

Singapura: "I'll just blow in the AOV's ear, and he'll do it." (AOV stands for Any Other Variety)

Siamese: "Make me!"

Birman: "Puh-leeez, dahling. I have servants for that kind of thing."

Maine coon: "Oh, me, me! Pleeeeeez let me change the lightbulb! Can I, huh? Can I? Huh? Huh? Can I?"

Exotic: "Let the AOV do it. You can feed me while he's busy."

Manx: "Why change it? I can wet on the carpet in the dark."

Russian blue: "While it's dark, I'm going to sleep on the couch."

Korat: "Korats are not afraid of the dark."

British shorthair: "Lightbulb? Lightbulb? That thing I ate was a lightbulb?"

Turkish angora: "You need light to see?"

British moggy: "None. Catnap time is too precious to waste!"

🐾 🐾 🐾

Cat Terminology

acceleration: A cat will accelerate at a constant rate until the cat gets good and ready to stop.

aerodynamics: If it flies, a cat will chase it.

bag or box occupancy: All open bags and boxes in a room must contain a cat within the earliest possible nanosecond.

dinner table attendance: A cat will attend all meals when anything good is served.

disinterest: A cat's interest level will vary in inverse proportion to the amount of effort a human expends trying to interest the cat.

electric blanket attraction: Turn on an electric blanket, and a cat will jump into bed at the speed of light.

elongation: A cat can make its body long enough to reach just about any countertop that has anything remotely interesting on it.

embarrassment: A cat's irritation rises in direct proportion to the cat's embarrassment multiplied by the amount of human laughter.

energy conservation (first law): A cat knows that energy can neither be created nor be destroyed and will therefore use as little energy as possible.

energy conservation (second law): A cat knows

that energy can be stored only by a lot of napping.

fluid displacement: A cat immersed in milk will displace its own volume, minus the amount of milk consumed.

furniture replacement: A cat's desire to scratch furniture is directly proportional to the cost of the furniture.

gravity: The cat knows that gravity works, even when sound asleep.

inertia: A cat at rest will tend to remain at rest unless acted upon by some outside force, such as the opening of cat food or a nearby scurrying mouse.

landing: A cat will always land in the softest place possible.

magnetism: Blue blazers and black sweaters attract cat hair in direct proportion to the darkness of the fabric.

milk consumption: A cat will drink its weight in milk, squared, just to show you that it can do it.

motion: A cat will move in a straight line unless there is a really good reason to change direction.

obedience resistance: A cat's resistance varies

in direct proportion to a human's desire for the cat to do something.

obstruction: A cat will lay on the floor in such a position as to obstruct the maximum amount of human foot traffic.

pill rejection: Any pill given to a cat has the potential energy to reach escape velocity.

random comfort seeking: A cat will always seek (and usually take over) the most comfortable spot in any room.

refrigerator observation: If a cat watches a refrigerator long enough, someone will come along and take out something good to eat.

rug configuration: No rug may remain in its naturally flat state.

sleeping: A cat will sleep with people whenever possible, in a position as uncomfortable for the people involved as possible, while maintaining the cat's own comfort.

stretching: A cat will stretch to a distance pro-portional to the length of the nap just taken.

thermodynamics: Heat flows from a warmer to a cooler body, except in the case of a cat, in which case all heat flows to the cat.

total composition: A cat is composed of matter, antimatter, and it doesn't matter!

Weather Conditions

1. To tell the weather, go to your back door and look for the dog.

2. If the dog is at the door and he is wet, it's probably raining. But if the dog is standing there really soaking wet, it is probably raining really hard.

3. If the dog's fur looks like it's been rubbed the wrong way, it's probably windy.

4. If the dog has snow on his back, it's probably snowing.

5. Of course, to be able to tell the weather like this, you have to leave the dog outside all the time, especially if you expect bad weather.

Sincerely,
The Cat

Purr-litical Correctness

My cat does not barf hair balls; he is a floor redecorator.

My cat does not break things; she helps gravity do its job.

My cat does not fear dogs; they are merely sprint practice tools.

My cat does not gobble; she eats with alacrity.

My cat does not scratch; he ventilates furniture, rugs, and skin.

My cat does not yowl; he sings off-key.

My cat is not a shedding machine; she is a hair relocation stylist.

My cat is not a "treat-seeking missile"; she enjoys the proximity of food.

My cat is not a bed hog; he is a mattress appreciator.

My cat is not a chatterbox; she is advising me on what to do next.

My cat is not a dope addict; she is catnip appreciative.

My cat is not a lap fungus; he is bed selective.

My cat is not a pest; she is attention deprived.

My cat is not a ruthless hunter; she is a wildlife control expert.

My cat is not evil; she is badness enhanced.

My cat is not fat; he is mass enhanced.

My cat is not hydrophobic; she has an inability to appreciate moisture.

My cat is not lazy; he is motivationally challenged.

My cat is not underfoot; she is shepherding me to my next destination (the food dish).

Cat Dictionary

miaowbu: Feed me.

meow: Pet me.

miioo-oo-oo: I am in love and must meet my betrothed outside beneath the hedge. Don't wait up.

mrow: I feel like making noise.

rrrow-mawww: Time to tidy the cat box.

rrrow-miawww: I have remedied the cat-box untidiness by shoveling the contents as far out of the box as was practical.

miaowmiaow: Play with me.

miaowmaww: Have you noticed the shortage of available cat toys in this room?

miowoww: I can find nothing to play with, so I'll see what happens when I sharpen my claws on this handy piece of furniture.

raowwwww: I will now spend time licking the most private parts of my anatomy.

mrowwwww: Some of my private parts did not return with me from that visit to the vet.

roww-maww-roww: I am so glad to see that you have returned home with both arms full of groceries. I will now rub myself against your legs and attempt to trip you as you walk toward the kitchen.

gakk-ak-ak: My digestive passages seem to have formed a hair ball. Where could this have come from? I will leave it here on the carpet.

mow: Snuggling is a good idea.

mowwow: Shedding is pretty good too.

mowww: I was enjoying snuggling and shedding in the warm, clean laundry until you so unkindly removed me.

miaow, miaow: I have discovered that, although one may be able to wedge his body through the gap behind the stove and into that little drawer filled with pots and pans, the reverse path is slightly more difficult to navigate.

mraakk: Oh, small bird! Please come over here.

ssssRoww: I believe that I have found a wood-chuck or similar animal.

mmmrowmmm: The best-tasting fish is one you have caught yourself.

mmmmmmm: If I sit in the sunshine for another hour or so, I think I'll be satisfied.

mreoaw: Please ask room service to send up another can of tuna.

mreeeow: Do you serve catnip with that?

mroow: I have forced my body into a tiny space in order to look cute. How am I doing?

miaooww, mriaow: You are using the can opener, so you must understand the value of a well-fed and pampered cat. Please continue.

🐾 🐾 🐾

"That's the fruitcake Mother gave us."

Does Your Cat Own You?

Do you select your friends based on how well your cats like them?

Does your desire to collect cats intensify during times of stress?

Do you buy more than 50 pounds of cat litter a month?

Do you scoop out the litter box after each use? Do you wait at the box with the scoop in your hand?

Do you think your cat is cute when it swings on the drapes or licks the butter?

Do you admit to non–cat owners how many cats you really have?

Do you sleep in the same position all night because your cat is annoyed when you move?

Do you kiss your cat on the lips?

Do you feed your cat tidbits from the table with your fork?

Does your cat sit at the table (or *on* the table) when you eat?

Does your cat sleep on your head? Do you like it?

Do you have more than four opened but rejected cans of cat food in the refrigerator?

Do you watch bad TV because the cat is sleeping on the remote?

Do you play videos of fish swimming in an aquarium to entertain your cat?

Do you stand at the open door indefinitely in the freezing rain while your cat sniffs the door, deciding whether to go out or come in?

Would you rather spend a night at home with your cat than go out on a mediocre date?

Do you give your cat presents and a stocking at Christmas? Do you spend more for your cat than you do for your spouse?

Do the Christmas cards you send out feature your cat sitting on Santa's lap? Does your cat sign the card?

Do you put off making the bed until the cat gets up?

Does your cat eat out of cut crystal stemware because you both watched the same commercial on television?

Do you microwave your cat's food? Prepare it from scratch?

Do you climb out of bed over the headboard or footboard so you won't disturb the cat?

At the store, do you pick up the cat food and kitty litter before you pick out anything for yourself?

Do you cook a special turkey for your cat on holidays?

Does your cat insist on a fancy Sunday breakfast consisting of an omelette made from eggs, milk, and either salmon, halibut, or trout?

Do you have pictures of your cat in your wallet? Do you bring them out when your friends share pictures of their children? (Pollsters claim that 40 percent of cat owners carry their pets' pictures in their wallets, by the way.)

When people call to talk to you on the phone, do you insist that they say a few words to your cat as well?

Do you accept dates only with those who have a cat? If so, do you eventually double-date with the cats to see how they get along?

When someone new comes to your house, do you introduce your cat to them by name?

🐾 🐾 🐾

Ten Things a Cat Thinks About

1. I could have sworn I heard the can opener.

2. Is there something I'm not getting when humans make noise with their mouths?

3. Why doesn't the government do something about dogs?

4. I wonder...did Morris really like 9-Lives, or did he have ulterior motives?

5. Hmmm...if dogs serve humans, and humans serve cats, why can't we cats ever get these stupid dogs to do anything for us?

6. This looks like a good spot for a nap.

7. Hey! No kidding, I'm sure that's the can opener.

8. Would humans have built a vast and complex civilization of their own if we cats hadn't given them reasons to invent sofas and can openers in the first place?

9. If God exists, how can He allow neutering?

10. If that really was the can opener, I'll play finicky just to let them know who's boss.

Things Cats Must Try to Remember

- Screaming at the can of food will not make it open itself.

- I should not assume the patio door is open when I race outside to chase leaves.

- If I put a live mouse in my food bowl, I should not expect it to stay there until I get hungry.

- The guinea pig likes to sleep once in a while. I will not watch him constantly.

- If I bite the cactus, it will bite back.

- I will not stand on the bathroom counter, stare down the hall, and growl at nothing right after my human has finished watching *The X-Files*.

- Television and computer screens do not exist to backlight my lovely tail.

- Regardless of how dangly and attractive they are, my human's earrings are not cat toys.

- If I play "dead cat on the stairs" while people are trying to bring in groceries or laundry, one of these days it will really come true.

- My human is capable of cooking bacon and eggs without my help.

- The canned cat food is already dead. I do not need to kill it by swatting bits of it all over the floor.

- I am a carnivore. Potted plants are not meat.

- I will never be able to walk on the ceiling, and staring up the wall and screaming at it will not bring it any closer.

- It is not a good idea to try to lap up the powdered creamer before it all dissolves in the boiling coffee.

- The goldfish likes living in water and must be allowed to remain in its bowl.

- If my human wants to share her sandwich with me, she will give me a piece. She will notice if I start eating it from the other end.

- I cannot leap through closed windows to catch birds outside.

- The large dog in the backyard has lived there for six years. I will not freak out every time I see it.

- I am a neutered cat, not a peacock, and prancing around with my tail fluffed up will not make my parts grow back.

- If I must give a present to my humans overnight guests, my toy mouse is much more socially acceptable than a live cockroach, even if it isn't as tasty.

🐾 🐾 🐾

Signs Your Cat Has Learned Your Internet Password

- You get e-mail flames from some guy named Fluffy.

- You find traces of kitty litter in your keyboard.

- You find you've been subscribed to strange newsgroups like www.alt.recreational.catnip.org

- Your Web browser has a new home page at CalicoScootz.com.

- Your mouse has teeth marks in it—and a strange aroma of tuna.

- Your sent items box includes hate-mail messages to Apple about their release of CyberDog.

- Your new ergonomic keyboard has a strange territorial scent to it.

- You keep finding new software around your house like CatTax and WarCat II.

- Your instant-messaging username is Iron-Mouser.

- You see little kitty carpal-tunnel braces near the scratching post.

Other Books by Bob Phillips

*All-Time Awesome Collection
of Good Clean Jokes for Kids*

*The Awesome Book
of Bible Trivia*

*Awesome Good Clean
Jokes for Kids*

*Awesome Knock-Knock
Jokes for Kids*

*The Best of the Good
Clean Jokes*

Bible Trivia for Every Day

Dude, Got Another Joke?

*Extremely Good Clean
Jokes for Kids*

*Fabulous and Funny
Clean Jokes for Kids*

*Flat-Out Awesome Knock-Knock
Jokes for Kids*

*Good Clean Jokes to Drive Your
Parents Crazy*

*Good Clean Knock-Knock
Jokes for Kids*

Jolly Jokes for Older Folks

*Nutty Knock-Knock
Jokes for Kids*

Over the Hill & On a Roll

*Over the Next Hill
& Still Rolling*

*Over the Top Clean
Jokes for Kids*

*Super Incredible Knock-Knock
Jokes for Kids*

*The World's Greatest
Collection of Clean Jokes*

*The World's Greatest
Knock-Knock Jokes for Kids*

---

*Other Books by Bob Phillips
and Jonny Hawkins*

*The Awesome Book
of Cat Humor*

*The Awesome Book
of Dog Humor*

*The Awesome Book
of Heavenly Humor*

*Laughter from
the Pearly Gates*

Other Books by Jonny Hawkins

Fishing Cartoon-a-Day Calendar

Medical Cartoon-a-Day Calendar

Car 'Toon-a-Day Calendar